6

COACH YOURSELF
BETTER, FAST

REIMAGINE
YOUR CAREER

Based on *Work/Life Flywheel*
by Ollie Henderson

First published in Great Britain by Practical Inspiration Publishing, 2025

© Ollie Henderson and Practical Inspiration Publishing, 2025

The moral rights of the author have been asserted.

ISBN   978-1-78860-750-6   (paperback)
        978-1-78860-751-3   (epub)
        978-1-78860-752-0   (Kindle)

All rights reserved. This book, or any portion thereof, may not be reproduced without the express written permission of the publisher.

Every effort has been made to trace copyright holders and to obtain their permission for the use of copyright material. The publisher apologizes for any errors or omissions and would be grateful if notified of any corrections that should be incorporated in future reprints or editions of this book.

EU GPSR representative: LOGOS EUROPE, 9 rue Nicolas Poussin, LA ROCHELLE 17000, France Contact@logoseurope.eu

Want to bulk-buy copies of this book for your team and colleagues? We can customize the content and co-brand *Reimagine your Career* to suit your business's needs.

Please email info@practicalinspiration.com for more details.

Practical Inspiration Publishing™

Contents

Series introduction iv
Introduction: The Work/Life Flywheel 1
Day 1: Your work revolution 3
Day 2: Reinvention 10
Day 3: Mindset: horizons and stars 29
Day 4: Visualization and prioritization 41
Day 5: Creativity: magic and flow 51
Day 6: Experimentation: design and test 67
Day 7: Community: connecting
and collaborating 82
Day 8: Ongoing success 93
Day 9: Time to pause 106
Day 10: Tracking, trusting and taking steps 120
Conclusion: sharing your ideas 130
Endnotes 132

Series introduction

Welcome to *6-Minute Smarts*!

This is a series of very short books with one simple purpose: to introduce you to ideas that can make life and work better, and to give you time and space to think about how those ideas might apply to your life and work.

Each book introduces you to ten powerful ideas, but ideas on their own are useless – that's why each idea is followed by self-coaching questions to help you work out the 'so what?' for you in just six minutes of exploratory writing. What's exploratory writing? It's the kind of writing you do just for yourself, fast and free, without worrying what anyone else thinks. It's not just about getting ideas out of your head and onto paper where you can see them, it's about finding new connections and insights as you write. This is where the magic happens.

Find out more...

Introduction: The Work/Life Flywheel

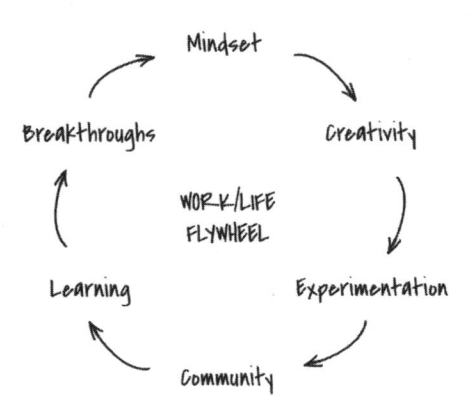

```
         Mindset
       ↗         ↘
Breakthroughs    Creativity
    ↑    WORK/LIFE    ↓
         FLYWHEEL
  Learning       Experimentation
       ↖         ↙
         Community
```

The Work/Life Flywheel model will give you the confidence to propel forward into the next phase of your career. By adapting the model to reflect your motivations, personality and circumstances, you

1

can carve out your unique place within the world of work. The model will spark ideas and provoke new possibilities to help you build a complementary relationship between your work and personal life.

Combining physical activity with rest and recovery will supercharge your creativity. Curiosity leads to experimentation, and while there will be inevitable failures, these will help deepen understanding and accelerate your learning. Incorporating a creative approach into every aspect of your work/life will help you build the confidence to do your thinking in public.

The habits you build will allow you to embrace uncertainty and take control of your future by providing the momentum to continue creating and building.

Your work/life isn't neatly divided into distinct parts. It's messy and overlapping, but the Work/Life Flywheel will help you to prioritize how to spend your time and energy. The results are profound and life-changing!

You're ready to start. Over ten chapters (ten days, if you fancy treating this as a mini-course), you're going to discover ten key principles that will enable you to reimagine your career and experiment with using them for yourself.

Let's go!

Day 1
Your work revolution

The Covid-19 pandemic served as a seismic catalyst, challenging traditional work models and forcing a rapid shift in how millions of people approach their jobs. Only a few years ago, remote working was a peculiarity reserved for a handful of tech businesses, but now millions of people worldwide will never return to the office. The relationship between their work and personal lives has fundamentally changed.

We're in the middle of the greatest work/life transition ever.

Reimagining where, when, how and why we work

- If we're no longer constrained to the office, how about we reconsider *when* and *how* we work too?

- Could we monetize our skills and experience outside a conventional 9–5 job and 'go it alone'?

Since 2020, the rate of new company registrations in the UK and USA has accelerated. A new wave of entrepreneurship has emerged as so many explore the benefits of becoming free agents for the first time. But perhaps the most profound trend to emerge is a collective reassessment of our priorities in work and life.

As the pandemic put our lives on temporary hold, many people started wondering:

- Why are we wasting time commuting into an office *every day*?
- Why are we spending so much time in meetings?
- Why the hell do we do what we do anyway?!

The work revolution is empowering us to look for something more than just money and status.

How can we redesign work?

Lynda Gratton, in *Redesigning Work*, suggests that as people quickly adapted to the circumstances forced on them by the pandemic, they soon recognized the benefits of working more flexibly.[1] This has pushed people to force employers to think differently, starting with how we design jobs and where and when we're most productive. Millions are now weighing up whether to pursue an alternative path, not traditional employment.

What's changing?

Organizations now need to become more flexible in how they think about the make-up of their workforce. According to a 2021 McKinsey report on workplace trends, among the most important factors behind people's decisions about moving roles were:

- being valued by their manager
- feeling a sense of belonging
- having potential for advancement
- having a flexible work schedule

However, the best talent wasn't simply moving from one employer to another. An increasing number decided to leave full-time employment entirely and go it alone.

Why is this happening?

Flexibility in when and how you work isn't the only thing at play. A desire for more autonomy also applies, including choosing which clients you work for and what you do for them.

And, of course, financial considerations are significant.

Many freelancers still experience a sense of 'feast or famine' – either turning work away or scrabbling around for enough to pay the bills.

If this sounds familiar, don't worry. With a mindset shift and the right strategy, you can shift from a freelancer to a solopreneur, with a consistent stream of opportunities and a more diverse portfolio of work that produces passive income.

What does it mean for businesses?

While individuals can leverage their unique experience and expertise to increase their earnings potential, businesses can access high-calibre, specialized talent on a needs-only basis.

Tim Oldman, CEO of workplace insights firm Leesman, explained that their research showed clearly that the businesses that thrived during the uncertain and unpredictable pandemic period were those who responded flexibly and creatively.

A competitive advantage exists for organizations that recognize the opportunity and choose to embrace it. Meanwhile, a new generation of solopreneurs and entrepreneurs will have more control over their futures and can maximize their value in the market.

Let's dig into why now is the perfect time to make a transition.

So what? Over to you...

1. How would you design your work/life if you could start from scratch?

2. What do you prioritize most – security, flexibility, money or variety?

3. How can you take advantage of the work revolution to make big changes in your career?

Day 2
Reinvention

If it feels as if your life has been thrown up in the air over the past few years, don't worry – you're not the only one!

In his book *Life Is in the Transitions: Mastering change at any age*, Bruce Feiler introduces the concept of 'lifequakes', major events that reshape our lives and challenge our sense of purpose.[2]

Lifequakes may be involuntary (such as war, recession or a partner leaving you) or voluntary (like quitting your job to start a new business or to travel around the world). You may experience these major upheavals personally or collectively, and you may question your purpose or explore whether you're living the life you always dreamed of. How you react to these events, however, is critical.

This is where transitions come in.

Unlike lifequakes, which in some cases are out of our control, undergoing a transition is something we choose. Feiler describes this transitional process as having three parts, which are easily recognizable.

1. 'The long goodbye', when we come to terms with leaving the old person behind.
2. 'The messy middle', in which we ditch some habits and acquire new ones.
3. 'The new beginning', in which we redefine our story to reflect a new direction.

The involuntary, collective transition

When I first came across Feiler's book in May 2020, it touched a nerve. I wasn't alone – the pandemic became a lifequake for billions worldwide, prompting many to rethink their priorities and explore new paths to fulfillment.

Transitions are an opportunity to break bad habits and adopt new, more positive ones. The trick is introducing these changes incrementally and establishing routines that help you make progress and reinvigorate and rejuvenate you.

Reinventing ourselves

Let's now look at Beatrice Hackett, who after a decade of working in the City retrained as a coach and now specializes in supporting others through career transitions.

A key component of her coaching methodology is how you think about your sense of identity. You may define yourself by the work you do. If you decide to pivot careers, you'll be doing something new, and with that comes earning less money and, possibly, feeling like your status has reduced somehow. Once you've accepted that you're going through a transition, your focus can then switch to where you want to end up.

If you know that this is the time for a transition but have no idea how to get there, the Work/Life Flywheel model will help you explore the next chapter of your career and identify the incremental steps to progress.

Personalization at scale

It's worth considering how broader changes in the world of work can support a personal reinvention process. The personalization of jobs certainly hasn't kept pace with our experience as consumers. We expect to have our content curated based on our viewing habits on Netflix. Amazon customizes our shopfront. Our social feeds highlight the people we're most interested in following. Yet, our work experience remains strangely lodged in the past.

The *future* of work is personalized, meaning for the first time we'll have the opportunity to focus not just on what we're good at but on what we're passionate about too.

Thanks to the internet, you can now easily connect with someone on the other side of the world who shares your interests, however niche. 'Not everyone has unique skills and the get-up-and-go to monetize them', you might say. Well, this is where the Work/Life Flywheel comes in. By focusing on the things that bring us energy, developing a mindset of creativity and experimentation, and taking advantage of an expanding network, you can go from being uninspired to being driven in the pursuit of your objectives.

It's all about reframing what success looks like and leveraging technology to make it happen.

The passion economy

The digital world has created the scale which allows us to reimagine how we can combine our expertise with something we care about. Most of us have something about which we're passionate or knowledgeable – and in many cases, both. This passion economy presents an opportunity to share this with others and, crucially, *get paid for it*.

It's less a case of 'do what you love' and more 'love what you do'.

Whenever people talk about work in these terms, it's obligatory to caveat it with an acknowledgement that not everyone has this luxury. I get it. Some people don't have the same advantages growing up, and it's impossible for every individual to perfectly craft their work/lives and do a job they're passionate about.

Here's a note of optimism, though.

As the cost to access technology reduces and the internet continues to provide an unlimited reservoir of knowledge, learning resources and, crucially, audiences, new opportunities will emerge. Creating online gets easier every day, but creating unique content and sharing valuable ideas is difficult, which is why your starting point has to be a willingness to carve your own niche.

But what if it doesn't work out?

When the demands of your job have taken their toll, you may risk burn-out. That's what happened to Laura Price, so she changed jobs (and continents!) for a new life in Dublin, only to be diagnosed with cancer shortly afterwards. Encountering the fragility of life like this helped her redefine her priorities. Leaving behind her corporate career, she pursued her passion for writing, completing a novel – *Single Bald Female* – which allowed her to creatively inspire others with a fictional story sparked by her own experience of breast cancer.

For Laura, the financial uncertainty was far outweighed by the sense of fulfilment she gained from a work/life characterized by creativity, experimentation and constant learning – as she put it, 'it's the personal satisfaction of doing something that no one has *asked me to do*'.

The reasons holding you back

For you, hopefully, the reasons you're considering a work/life transition are less dramatic. Whether you're thinking about changing jobs, starting a new business or just setting time aside for that hobby you'd abandoned, now is the time to act.

At this point, it may still feel more like a dream than a reality. You may have dipped your toe in the water by starting a side project or moonlighting outside (or, shh, during!) working hours. If you're particularly bold, you may even have taken the plunge and quit your job.

The chances are, though, you haven't yet mustered up the courage to act.

You're not alone. The reality is that although many people want to make big changes, far fewer follow through.

Why?

Invariably, it comes down to fear of failure, which isn't a surprise when discussions about pivoting your career tend to focus on the risks – some real and some perceived.

Or you may have a mortgage and young children. You may be wondering how the financials of your potential new career direction stack up against the security of your employment contract and steady income. If it doesn't work, how will you pay the bills?

And how about the fact you've never done it before? If you've only ever worked for someone else, how will you know where to start when it comes to all the tasks unrelated to your skill set?

Another reason that frequently comes up in my research is reputational risk.

What will people think of me if I don't get it right? How will I look at myself in the mirror if I quit my successful job and try something that fails?

Reinvention

How to avoid regret

There are always reasons not to do something, but you're more likely to regret *inaction* than *action*. As Dan Pink explained to me on the *Future Work/Life* podcast, people often rue their failure to act boldly in their work and personal lives.

As a thought exercise, imagine yourself 20 years in the future, looking back on the decisions you make now. How would you feel if you didn't follow through when you're confident in your abilities, knowledge and capacity to learn? Back in the present, this 'what if?' question elicits the same insights every time: most people wish they'd spoken up more, made the jump into going it alone and set up the business they've always dreamed of.

Reframing our emotions

Use your emotions positively!

The work of Dr Kristin Neff, a psychology professor at the University of Texas, shows that people who demonstrate more 'self-compassion' are happier, more satisfied with life, better motivated and physically healthier. They also maintain stronger relationships and are less anxious, less prone to depression and more resilient.[3]

So how do we foster more self-compassion?

- Be kind to yourself and non-judgemental about the decisions you make.
- Recognize that making mistakes is 'human', and everyone experiences the same feeling at different points in their lives.
- Face up to failure and pain with equanimity – a calm, mindful acceptance that the world and your life is how it is, flaws and all.

I also spoke to Damian Hughes, organizational psychologist and co-host of the chart-topping *High Performance* podcast. He had become seriously ill due to his relentless pace of work. Damian was brutal in how he spoke to himself about the relentless need to keep pushing when he should have been taking a break and slowing down. But it was only after reflecting on how he'd view it if someone spoke to his son the way he talked to himself that he could gain perspective and break his damaging habits. Acknowledging and labelling your feelings helps unburden you from worries and can alleviate anxiety and lower the risk of depression.

If you're deliberating over a difficult choice, picture what you'd tell your best friend if they came to you with the same dilemma.

The answers are in there somewhere – you may just need to look at the question from a different viewpoint.

Talking to yourself

Talking about yourself to yourself helps reframe problems that seem insurmountable and gives you more confidence. You can also combine this with 'temporal distancing' – projecting your thoughts to the future, or back in time – to separate yourself from all-consuming short-term worries. For example, if you regretted making a bold choice about your career ten years ago, you can use that to inform your decision-making today.

Living in the future

It can take time to build the confidence to follow your own path and pursue a work/life that marries your passion with your expertise.

However, by approaching the process with the right mindset, and combining creativity and experimentation with the support of your community, you will be successful.

To perfectly balance work and life is impossible. For a start, how do you even measure that? Maybe when you're feeling unquestionably happy and fulfilled in both? Fair enough, but let's be honest, those moments can feel fleeting for many of us. Plus, it can be challenging to pinpoint precisely what changes from one day to the next, as your perception of achieving 'balance' shifts.

But if not balance, then what?

In *Parents Who Lead*, Stewart Friedman and Alyssa Westring wrote about how parents could take a more realistic approach to designing their work/lives, taking into account four common areas of life – work, home/family, community, self.[4]

They found that recognizing the connection between the four areas is critical to success and well-being. Embracing how they integrate with one another can empower you to feel greater purpose and harmony across all parts of your life.

Management frameworks

Well-known phrases such as 'FOMO' ('fear of missing out', coined by Patrick McGinnis) and

'MVP' ('minimum viable product', coined by Eric Ries) are adopted at scale because they succinctly capture an idea, mood or feeling. Add a metaphor to the equation and they become even more appealing, bringing to life otherwise abstract concepts.

The Flywheel Effect

The beauty of the flywheel is that with only a little explanation and framing, it becomes a lens through which you view every successful company and product.

Many founders and entrepreneurs may often feel as if they are pushing at a bloody great wheel with very little assistance. You just about manage to get the thing moving but not without a serious amount of strain and a large dollop of doubt about whether it's worth it. But you keep on pushing and by the second turn it becomes a little easier. By the tenth rotation, there's a sense that the wheel's weight, rather than impeding its progress, may actually be helping you move it.

If you stopped pushing here, the wheel would quickly grind to a halt, but by keeping the momentum up, the speed gradually increases and before you know it the wheel appears to be moving entirely on its own.

In a great business, no single part of the flywheel is more important than any other – they're interdependent. While the composition of each flywheel differs depending on the industry, customer need and expertise of the people activating the plan, the result is a virtuous circle of value creation.

Amazon's virtuous circle

Much as the compounding effect of interest ultimately leads to wealth creation, a good decision built on a good decision repeated many times over will propel a business to greatness.

Jeff Bezos and his team designed their own flywheel built on their obsession with creating customer value.

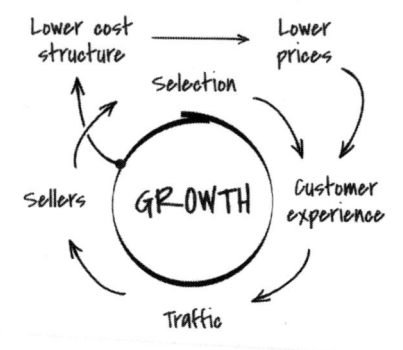

Amazon understood that increasing the number of shoppers required the removal of the friction caused by limited availability, cataloguing of products and clunky check-out processes. As traffic increased to the site, this brought an opportunity for Amazon to invite third parties to sell their products through the platform, creating an open marketplace rather than a traditional retailer model, and they were able to match supply with demand. All of this contributed to a constantly improving customer experience, completing the virtuous circle.

As with any business model flywheel, the model was constantly in motion, evolving and expanding. Lower cost structures meant they could lower their prices, further enhancing customer experience and making the flywheel spin even faster.

Your Work/Life Flywheel

While the individual components of each business flywheel are different, what's common to all of them is that no single part is any more important than any other, with everything working together in harmony. Each component feeds into the next until momentum builds between them and the virtuous circle is created. Although we all have unique characteristics, goals and talents, there are six building blocks common to every successful approach:

1. Mindset
2. Creativity
3. Experimentation
4. Community
5. Learning
6. Breakthroughs

So, where do we begin?

The first step is to develop a pragmatic *mindset* that focuses on being clear about your values and objectives.

Building on your intrinsic motivations and goals, focus on how they feed into adopting *creativity* as a core value. Creativity will be the differentiator in the future of work, so explore how to develop a habit of thinking differently and telling stories that matter to people.

Creativity demands that we accept that not everything we try will work out as planned, which is the next crucial part of the model. Developing an attitude of constant *experimentation* in our work/lives will unlock insight and help you establish your expert niche while exposing you to new and exciting opportunities and connections.

Reinvention

As an innovator, you need the support of others – your *community*. With the right combination of connections, and diverse knowledge and opinions, you'll discover that your speed of learning accelerates.

This helps you adopt a new approach to lifelong *learning*, which takes into account longer life expectancy and your work/life taking multiple paths as your career evolves.

To realize the benefits of everything you're doing, you need time to rest and recover, which is when you achieve *breakthroughs* that give you the intrinsic rewards and motivational boosts that feed your positive *mindset*.

And so the circle is complete, and the wheel spins again. And again. And again.

Excited? Me too. Let's stop talking about the theory and crack on.

So what? Over to you…

1. What are you ready to leave behind to create space for a new direction in your career?

2. What small, low-risk step can you take this week to test your curiosity or passion in a new area?

3. What small, meaningful action could you take today to build confidence and momentum toward your desired change?

Day 3
Mindset: horizons and stars

Think about the following two sentences:

- Some people have all the luck.
- You make your own luck in life.

They represent two completely different outlooks on life.

The first is a begrudging acceptance that life happens to us. The second acknowledges that we have agency over our choices and life's outcomes. Two people may face the same conditions and opportunities but experience entirely different outcomes.

According to Christian Busch (best-selling author and professor), openness to the unexpected is key to being lucky.

The hook

If serendipity – luckiness – is part of an intentional outlook on life, how can you get better at making your own luck?

Let's start with how you greet people. What's your go-to question when you meet someone new at a party? Mundane ordinary questions don't reveal much about the person you're speaking to and significantly reduce your chance of finding common ground. So, why not try something different, such as, 'What do you enjoy doing?' or 'What are you most excited about over the next three months?'

If you're on the receiving end of the 'What do you do?' question, on the other hand, don't just share what you do for work – give them a 'hook' by volunteering more information to give a sense of who you really are. This gives people the chance to learn more about you and to make connections between *your* interests and experiences and *theirs*. All it takes is to be open-minded!

Broadening your horizons

In order to broaden my horizons, I made a conscious decision to connect with new people every week, which was a radical change in my mindset. As well as overcoming my natural reluctance to network, I developed a mindset that embraced any new opportunity that arose.

A simple shift in attitude and behaviour has led to new collaborations, paid gigs and friendships that have opened my eyes to subjects I never even knew existed. They sparked new levels of creativity and, after ongoing experimentation, gave me new knowledge and countless breakthroughs that ultimately contributed to me writing this book. Crucially, these new experiences allowed me to experiment with what I wanted to do next in my career.

So keep your eyes open for the unexpected. Make connections between parts of your life that complement one another and create a virtuous circle.

For example, you might sit in weekly meetings with your team and reflect on the highlight of the previous week – it's great to recognize people's contributions and progress. But how about if everyone also shared something unexpected that happened? As well as reminding everyone that not everything goes exactly to plan in work or life, we'd learn something entirely different about everyone's role and their experience throughout the week.

What's more, encouraging people to think about unpredictability positively demonstrates the value of the unanticipated, even if things don't always work out. It's easy to write ourselves and others off after making mistakes or experiencing 'failures', yet by reframing these events as precursors to the next stage of our lives, we can turn them into lessons that define our future.

Whether you're inspired to make a real difference to the lives of others or take this opportunity to change your own, now's the time. If you're still wondering where to start, the answer lies in this question: what really matters to you?

Your north star

Shaun Tomson (world champion surfer) has merged his love of competition and pursuing the limits of human capability with an ethos of sharing and supporting one another.

In 2006, Shaun and his wife lost their 15-year-old son, Matthew, when a dangerous game went wrong. While life would never be the same, Shaun later reflected on how something he'd created several years before – The Surfers' Code – could inspire him to share a message of positivity and hope with others.

Mindset: horizons and stars

He gave a talk at a local school about how the kids could use The Code to help define how they wanted to live their lives. By asking them to start each sentence with 'I will', Shaun encouraged the children to think about committing to what they believed in.

The very first contribution he read was from a young girl who wrote: 'I will always be myself.'

This affected Shaun profoundly. He told me: 'I don't know whether my son played this game because of a peer pressure thing. Who knows? We'll never know, but those words spoke to me.... I started speaking at schools and getting kids to write their codes.'

Shaun's purpose is now to encourage people to identify their values, to encourage children to take the right path and, in doing so, to keep the spirit of his son alive. His north star – his overarching goal, which he continually uses to orientate himself in the right direction – is helping others find theirs.

How to live by your values

Your north star provides clarity and direction when progress feels stalled. But how do you stop yourself from compromising on your values? How would things change if you considered them as non-negotiable standards from which you'll never deviate? By stipulating the standards you'll stick to without fail, you're making your priorities clear to yourself, your family and friends, and the people you work with.

Commitment to anything in life requires making a choice – not just to pursue that goal, but to *ignore* the millions of other things that could take up the finite time you have available. By expressing the significance of your passion, you'll find a tribe of others that can relate. And it can often be the backing of these people that inspires and motivates you during those inevitable periods in work and life when progress seems to stall.

Kanter's law, a theory based on Rosabeth Moss Kanter's work,[5] describes how in the middle of any period of change – whether a work project, a career transition or becoming a parent – you'll experience a sense that everything is failing. It's precisely at this point that non-negotiables, and a crystal-clear focus on the outcomes you're aiming for, can help push you through. This is when you should think about your north star – when you're ready to pack it in and give up, a reminder and reassessment of your original purpose gives you fresh impetus.

In this scenario, ask yourself these questions:

Mindset: horizons and stars

- Are you still inspired by your vision for the future, and are those around you still willing to support you in achieving it?
- Can you identify progress you've already made, including tangible milestones and indicators that you're on the right track to succeed?
- Is there anything else you're doing that can help reignite your energy and reinvigorate your motivation?

In other words, during those inevitably tricky times we all experience, it helps to reaffirm that our destination is worth the struggle and the many small steps to get there. You can approach this in three distinct phases:

1. The outcome – your north star.
2. Measurable performance targets that show you're on the right track.
3. The everyday process to achieve these goals.

What to do if you're struggling

What might be preventing you from finding your purpose?

Could you be overcomplicating it?

Forget about identifying a worthy ideal and just focus on what you find interesting. We get so bogged down with the significance of 'discovering our purpose' that it often puts us off from even starting. Don't overthink it. Concentrate on things that you enjoy and make you feel good.

One approach I took was to use the Japanese idea of ikigai – 'the reason for being'.

Although the concept itself doesn't translate literally into English, it has been popularized by a Venn diagram focusing on four elements that make up a meaningful life:

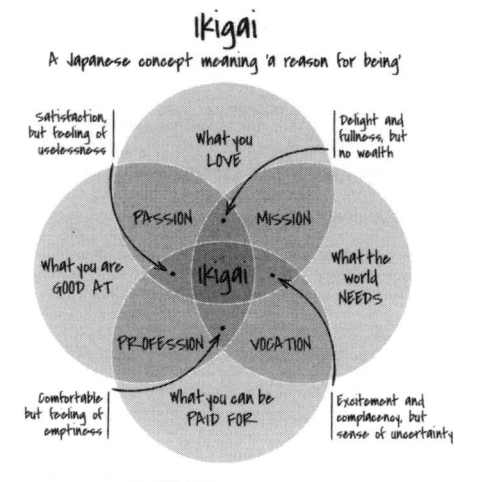

Ikigai
A Japanese concept meaning 'a reason for being'

- Satisfaction, but feeling of uselessness
- Delight and fullness, but no wealth
- What you LOVE
- PASSION
- MISSION
- What you are GOOD AT
- Ikigai
- What the world NEEDS
- PROFESSION
- VOCATION
- Comfortable but feeling of emptiness
- What you can be PAID FOR
- Excitement and complacency, but sense of uncertainty

Mindset: horizons and stars

- What you are good at
- What the world needs
- What you can be paid for
- What you love (the most important)

If you're missing any one part, then it's likely you won't be completely satisfied.

When I went through the exercise of identifying my ikigai in early 2020, it was transformative. I started by identifying the things that I love, then the things I'm good at, and then I mapped both of those against what the world needs and what people would be prepared to pay for. It helped me redesign my own work/life, and it can do the same for you.

So what? Over to you…

1. What specific actions could you take this week to increase openness to unexpected opportunities and 'make your own luck'?

Mindset: horizons and stars

2. What is your personal north star, and how might you use it to guide your decisions?

3. Have a go at drawing your own ikigai Venn diagram. What do you notice?

Day 4
Visualization and prioritization

What do you want to be when you grow up?

I'm sure you, like me, were asked that many times as a child. But is it a *good* question? We can rarely predict anyone's profession early in life. In fact, the idea of a 'profession' at all seems incredibly dated – a relic from a bygone era.

The question itself may not be wrong, but our expectations about the answer certainly are. What's important is that we focus on our *values* and what we want to *experience* in our work/lives. So rather than 'a footballer' or 'an astronaut', a more useful answer might be: 'I want to be constantly learning', or 'I want to be happy and grateful for the life and relationships I have.'

Once we've clarified our values, our priority should be making sure we follow through and spend our time on the right things.

The four-way view

Stewart Friedman and Alyssa Westring, experts in work/life integration, developed the Four-Way View model, which shows why an integrated approach to our work/life is the only realistic way to manage its complexity.[6] It looks at whether you spend your time on the things you really care about and, crucially, how that aligns with other significant people in your life.

The first step is to imagine the things you'll be doing as part of a happy, purposeful life.

Imagine it's 15 to 20 years from now:

- What do you do when you wake up in the morning? Are you getting out of bed and exercising? Meditating for half an hour? Snoozing some more? Going for a walk?
- What are you doing during the day? Are you still doing the job you love today? Spending your morning on a hobby? Volunteering?
- What does the end of your day look like? Are you congregating for a family meal? Working

Visualization and prioritization

on a series of passion projects? Sitting quietly with a book?

Visualizing the future can be a valuable and positive reminder of why we're doing 'this' now (whatever 'this' is).

Back in the present, you need to look objectively at how you're spending your time, which is where the four dimensions of your work/life come in:

1. Yourself
2. Your career
3. Your family
4. Your community

Are you spending your time right?

Here's an easy exercise you can do to determine how you'd spend your time in an ideal world and how you're doing right now:

1. Create a simple table, noting down the percentage of your waking hours that you'd like to dedicate to each of the four areas.
2. After spending 15 to 20 minutes reviewing your calendar, create another table in which you add how much time you actually spend on each.

3. If you have a partner, ask them to do this separately; then compare notes.

What's the objective?

- To assess whether you're meeting your time aspirations
- To discover which parts of your life are getting more or less attention than they deserve
- To give you a starting point to begin designing your time differently
- To ensure you and your family are on the same page about your respective values

This last part is essential because making big changes in your work/life is challenging, and you need the support of the people you care about.

I've identified my five non-negotiable values, which determine where I focus my energy:

1. Autonomy
2. Creativity
3. Curiosity
4. Growth
5. Humour

Visualization and prioritization

As well as giving you insight into how you spend your time, this exercise may also reveal why you're not as satisfied in your career as you'd like. If you're spending more time at work than you'd like *and* you're in a job you're not enjoying, that's a recipe for misery.

Visualizing your goals

So, you've established what matters most and where you'd like to focus your time. Now you need to work out how to get there by setting goals.

But how do you do that?

Start with the end in mind

The main challenge is recognizing the contribution of the work you do every day. To visualize the goal means bringing it closer, or better put, splitting the goal into small pieces and tackling each in turn.

Since it's so difficult to connect our choices today with something that won't pay off until many years in the future, we often don't follow through on the goals we set.

Foreshadowing failure

So what should you do to visualize yourself in the future? The secret is pairing positive visualization with what psychologists call 'foreshadowing of failure'. Simply put, you have to plan for what could go wrong. What could prevent you from reaching your goals?

To maximize your chances of achieving your goals, you need to picture yourself in your ideal future without forgetting to consider the obstacles that might prevent you from getting there.

- Be specific about how you'll judge success, and do this *before* you start the process.
- Use objective milestones to measure how you're performing, and don't forget to review these! (Track your progress in a journal, as writing it down produces a visual manifestation of what could otherwise get lost in the messiness of our busy lives.)

The importance of aiming high

There's a difference between creating a list of daily or weekly tasks and identifying your life and career goals. Yes, your day-to-day work helps you get

Visualization and prioritization

where you want to go, but how do you set that big target to aim at? It can be easy to think 'what's the point in even setting goals when plans so frequently change and life can often feel uncertain?'. So it's important to remember that our performance rises to the level of well-defined and appropriately judged goals, such as:

- **Align:** Agree a vision and then make improvements.
- **Promise:** Reprioritize your time to focus on your primary goal.
- **Increase:** Set a stretch goal.
- **Frame:** Agree a specific, substantial and measurable goal.

Now let's turn to another vital skill that you'll need to nurture to achieve your ambitions: creativity.

So what? Over to you…

1. How do your daily habits and relationships align with your ideal work/life 15 years from now?

Visualization and prioritization

2. Where are the biggest gaps between how you want to spend your time and how you actually spend it?

3. What might be a helpful stretch goal for you right now?

Day 5
Creativity: magic and flow

We can all be creative if we follow our curiosity and focus on things we genuinely care about. Creativity fuels innovation and problem-solving, and it connects us to a deeper sense of purpose. By tapping into our creative potential, we can transform the way we approach our work/life.

As technology and automation change the nature of jobs over the coming decades, the defining contribution of humans to business and society will be characteristics like creativity, context and critical thinking.

The magic of creativity

Nurturing a creative mindset is exciting, especially when you wake up every morning knowing that you have the opportunity to produce ideas that no one has ever thought of. Creativity is a state of mind, a willingness to think differently about problems and solutions.

Recognizing the creativity of others

A creative lifestyle means immersing yourself in the creativity of others too, because this inspires action. This is why reading fiction is important! Recent research from neuroscientists has shown that reading literary fiction builds empathy, improves critical thinking and opens the mind more effectively to other viewpoints. It supports the development of in-demand skills that are typically hard to teach – such as flexibility and adaptability, creative problem-solving and judgement.

So, never forget the value of transcending the here and now and seeing life through someone else's eyes. It's important to keep an open mind as that improves decision-making and avoids 'cognitive closure' (when you are more likely to struggle to change your mind as new information arises).

Personal branding

Personal branding is not just a way to promote yourself – it's an opportunity to creatively express your unique strengths and values. By asking yourself 'What value am I generating for others?', you can craft a personal narrative that resonates and inspires.

Hustle no more

It's easy to project the idea of 'hustling' with an appearance of hyper-productivity. But none of this is of any use if you're not creating anything of value to yourself or others. The ancient philosopher Aristotle even advocated being active and using our time and energy to grow and become a better person who gives more to others.

What's more, constantly focusing on yourself can be detrimental to personal growth. If you're concerned that you've been infected with 'Me Disease', take time to pause, step back and consider why you're doing what you're doing. Think about why someone should spend their time consuming something – what's in it for them?

Find your flow

Flow is where creativity thrives. During moments of deep concentration, your mind effortlessly connects ideas and generates solutions, making creativity an intrinsic part of the experience. When we're 'in flow', our sense of self vanishes, and our perception of time changes. The whole experience is intensely, intrinsically rewarding.

Operating under constraints

The reality of life can often get in the way of high performance at work, especially when you have young kids. But since flow state is a spectrum, I figured I could still benefit from some of the positive effects even if there were parts of my life that proved restrictive. Besides, if you can master the ability to drop into flow, you can do more in less time. If I could optimize in some areas, could I extract the benefits of achieving flow more consistently?

Well, it turns out I could. I just needed the right triggers.

22 flow triggers

The 22 flow triggers listed below are broken down into four categories: internal, external, creative and social. Think about each of the triggers as dials you can turn up. If all the dials are low, you can get into flow, but it won't be too intense. However, the higher the level of each trigger, the deeper your experience of the state of flow and the greater its benefits will be.

Internal

1. Autonomy
2. The triad of curiosity, passion and purpose
3. Complete concentration
4. Clear goals
5. Immediate feedback
6. The challenge–skills balance

External

7. High consequences
8. Novelty
9. Unpredictability
10. Complexity
11. Deep embodiment

Creative

12. Creativity, including building a pattern recognition system, thinking differently and treating creativity as a virtue

Social

13. Complete concentration
14. Shared, clear goals
15. Shared risk
16. Close listening
17. Good communication
18. Blending egos
19. Equal participation
20. Familiarity
21. A sense of control
22. Always saying yes

Developing our ability to enter a flow state helps realize gains in productivity, learning rate and, crucially, creativity. Here's how...

Internal triggers

When we're in charge of our mind (freedom of thought) and our destiny (freedom of choice), our

Creativity: magic and flow

whole being gets involved. So, continually returning to the exercise of clarifying what we're deeply interested in, what we're passionate about *and* why we're doing it is vital. As you think about the various tasks you work on during the week, start reflecting on how much they represent each of these three elements of intrinsic motivation.

You'll see that the more each of these elements show up, the easier it is to focus and perform at your best.

Use this simple three-step checklist:

1. Can you achieve everything you need with a pen, some paper and/or a single browser window or app?
2. Have you told everyone who might need to contact you that you're unavailable unless it's an emergency?
3. Have you placed all unnecessary devices out of reach or in another room?

In an ideal world, you'll create a period of 90–120 minutes without interruption. When you do this consistently and focus on the right things (which is where *clear* goals come in) combined with honest feedback from others, the uplift in performance means you'll deliver *more high-quality work in less time*.

This does, though, rely on one crucial factor – the *challenge–skills balance*. Finding the right level between the challenge of the task at hand and your *perceived* ability to do it is by far the most important flow trigger of all. So, what's the right balance, and how do we measure it?

Always aim to be stretched, but not to the point of snapping. If the task's too easy, you'll get bored. Too complex, and you'll become anxious.

Remember, the overall objective here is to improve performance, and in much the same way as you get your Work/Life Flywheel turning, the way to achieve this is by progressing a little more each time.

External triggers

When the level of risk is elevated, you create the optimal conditions for flow because the stakes are high – think about that important meeting or when you've taken an exam.

Likewise, external complexity can be a positive factor. This might involve breaking free of the usual routine or working in a completely new setting. If you can't actually base yourself somewhere else, don't worry – you can achieve similar results by going for a walk in nature before a session, for example. A change of scene really makes a difference.

During moments when you are completely immersed in a practical task, like gardening, you reduce your cognitive load, connect more deeply to your body and detach yourself from the 'thinking mind'. If you're wondering how to achieve the same result while sitting in front of a computer screen writing a report, or before stepping into an important presentation, don't worry – there's a decent workaround: mindfulness.

Deep embodiment is all about being in the moment. By paying close attention to your breath, you also become more aware of sound, touch, sight and smell, replicating the effects of a more physically sensory experience.

Creative triggers

Creativity is first and foremost about noticing connections between things in new ways. You need courage to achieve creative results consistently and share those ideas with others. All this relies on having a large bank of knowledge from which to draw. Designing your work/life to allow for ongoing learning gives you the toolkit to approach problems from new angles.

Stories, for example, can help you understand yourself and engage others. They can engage people in the moment and are the most effective tool to get your point across and make it stick.

Neuroeconomist Paul Zak identifies three crucial characteristics of a good story well told[7]:

1. Quickly develops tension
2. Shares the characters' emotions
3. Focuses on a single important idea

Achieve all three and you'll sustain your audience's attention and get your point heard.

How to use stories to reimagine your career

But how does recognizing the value of stories relate to your decisions about changes you're making in your career? Stories help explain what's possible, which matters when talking about something someone else cares about. To reimagine your career, you must first address *why* you want a change before crafting the story to help you achieve it.

Creativity: magic and flow

Start by being honest with yourself and those close to you about what's motivating you to change your work/life and what might be holding you back. Tell yourself your own story, starting with how you came to this point and what the future will look like for you. Be honest about your worries, hopes and what you believe in.

Next, consider your work story.

- What's held you back in your career so far, and how are you overcoming these obstacles?
- As you reimagine your career, what does the next phase look like?
- How will you prioritize your time, and how will you feel as you begin making progress towards your goals?

To be truly effective, you have to be specific about the new future you're trying to create and bring it to life. Tell your story about what your future looks like, how you and other people will feel and what that feeling will empower you to do.

Mastering storytelling allows you to create powerful new ways to share your ideas and persuade others to join you on your mission.

How to tell your story

How can you craft a story whenever you need it, to help motivate yourself and others? Well, it just takes work – a consistent, structured approach to collecting stories.

As well as making a short note of daily highlights before bed each night, I began recording one or two 'notable' stories or events that happened during the day. I'd occasionally return to this list and experience a magical feeling of being transported back in time to that moment. I found it improved my memory – amazing!

My sense of time has changed. Whereas life has increasingly felt like it's flashing by before my eyes, documenting significant and memorable events has created a feeling that time is slowing down.

I can remember every day in my life. It's a revelation!

Free-writing

There's one more technique that I'd love you to try.

Start without any preconceived notions of what you want to achieve and jot down whatever comes into your head. Matthew Dicks calls this 'dreaming

Creativity: magic and flow

at the end of your pen'.[8] By recording every memory that emerges within ten minutes, you'll recall events that you haven't thought about for years. Good or bad, these are likely the stories that have formed your personality and beliefs. They present opportunities for you to contextualize decisions you make in the future, including decisions about how to influence others to join you on the next stage of your journey.

There's one indisputable fact about your life – you're the only one living it. Having more agency over the direction it takes requires you becoming the author of your own story. So, slow down and capture some of these unique moments.

✏️ So what? Over to you…

1. What specific problem or challenge in your work/life could you reframe creatively to uncover a new solution or perspective?

Creativity: magic and flow

2. How can you design your work/life to include more opportunities for flow and focus, despite your constraints?

3. What story are you currently telling yourself about your career, and how might you rewrite it to reflect the future you want to create?

Day 6
Experimentation: design and test

As soon as asynchronous work – people collaborating in different places at varying times – became commonplace during Covid-19, it was like a light bulb lit up for millions worldwide. Not only can you get more done when you're working on your own in a distraction-free environment, but you can now work for any organization, anywhere in the world.

But asynchronous work demands new, improved communication skills, and first among them is the ability to articulate your message through writing clearly.

With mass digital connectivity, the rules have changed, and we've all got the opportunity to engage our 'tribe' if we approach the process with discipline and learn lessons from the best.

How to get started

There are pros and cons to the internet. One of the downsides of social media is that there's a permanent record of everything you do. On the other hand, you can learn how others have achieved success. And a vital place to start is figuring out why you're doing it – otherwise, you'll never be able to measure your progress.

So:

- What do you want to achieve?
- What's the perfect outcome?

Just as most people are afraid of making big changes in their careers, they're also afraid of putting themselves out there online, so it takes courage to stand out. Being known for something specific makes you the go-to person whenever someone needs that problem solved, so embrace it!

Combining your career with your passion

Take Phil Askew, Creative Director of a successful agency. He found there was no further opportunity

Experimentation: design and test

for career progression, so he went to see a coach to help him navigate a change. A decade on, he had established a reputation as a coach of coaches. But he still felt like something was missing, and he realized he wasn't following his own advice.

Creativity had literally been his job for many years, but he'd parked his natural curiosity with his old job as he established his coaching business and expertise. He had his 'aha' moment only after walking himself through the ikigai process (see Day 3), which he'd typically use with clients. 'I love photography, and I love taking photos of people, but I wasn't doing it at all. That's when I made the decision to incorporate it into my work.'

Phil had to create a new niche, and his communication skills and the visual power of his photos have allowed him to develop a proposition that excites his customers and, crucially, himself. Being known for something specific is a career accelerant, and when you connect that with something you're genuinely interested in, it's a recipe for fulfilment and growth.

Naming and claiming your niche

Going niche feels uncomfortable at first as you wrestle with thinking that people won't be interested in something so specific. But experiment to find your niche and remember that you don't have to stick with it for the rest of your life. The secret is to find something that resonates with you and the people you're talking to. This will require some testing.

Designing tests

The seed of doubt which lingers inside you can potentially be crippling and prevent you from progressing in your career and making positive decisions about work and life.

Having interviewed so many incredibly bright and successful people, I find what's reassuring is the honesty with which many of them approach subjects like imposter syndrome.

In his book, *Alive At Work*, Dan Cable discusses the concept of 'humble leadership', which works by recognizing that no one's perfect and that the only path to success is through experimentation, learning, failing and improving.[9]

Why is learning so important in this case? Well, if you accept that you're always learning, it makes failing not just acceptable but necessary. As Glen Elliot told me: 'Innovation, by definition, *has to have a significant chance of failure*. Otherwise, it's just

Experimentation: design and test

something that someone else has done – it's not innovative.'

Don't fail fast, learn fast

In 2006, Joe Gebbia and Brian Chesky launched a new website, which they'd designed to allow locals to rent out their spare beds while large conferences were taking place nearby.

Soon afterwards, they discovered that people found it awkward exchanging money in person, and their new business idea stalled. The two designers quickly began testing online payments, and they immediately saw a spike in new users. So, the first iteration of the (yes, you guessed it!) Airbnb offering didn't work. So is 'failure' a fair description?

No!

They 'learned fast'. Experimentation means acknowledging that you rarely nail it first time round. However, it also depends on creating a structure that ensures 'failure' is never catastrophic.

So, if the objective is to learn, how do you design an experiment to optimize doing this quickly?

Testing hypotheses

It's important to design experiments that consistently deliver actionable insights, irrespective of the results.

That means we need to ask the right questions in advance:

- What are your underlying assumptions about the problem you're trying to solve?
- How will these assumptions play out?
- What effects might they have on the business or, for that matter, your work/life?

The discipline of establishing a hypothesis forces you to think about both the desired outcome and possible reasons for failure – what some people call a 'pre-mortem'. Ensuring that the experiment is measurable ensures you have something against which to judge success. For example, if your assumption is that offering short coaching sessions will attract more clients, you might test this by promoting a 'mini-session' package for one month and analyzing the response rate.

Focus on what you can control

The nature of experiments is that they don't always work. Concentrate on what you can control.

Experimentation: design and test

- What are your guiding principles?
- How can you test whether you're making progress to achieving this objective?
- What can you test that's within *your* control?
- Can you keep your core values and mission in mind whenever you're experimenting?

As long as you don't beat yourself up when things don't go right the first time, you'll find yourself enjoying how quickly you learn from the results of your tests.

Starting new projects often depends on doing new things and learning on the job. Keep that long-term vision in mind, and ensure your experiments are measurable. The question is then the scale of the test. There are times for taking large, calculated risks like pivoting your company or career, but you only do it when you're basing the decision on an informed judgement. Otherwise, you should start by making smaller bets. Ask yourself these questions:

1. What's the itch that you want to scratch?
2. Why do you think that it presents an opportunity?
3. What's the worst that can happen if it flops?

Let's look at how to design a content flywheel that works for you.

The content flywheel

Now that everyone can access facts with a Google search, it's no longer about what you know but *how you communicate ideas*. Are you ready to think in public?

Public thinking

Most people never engage in public thinking (which I'm using as shorthand for speaking at conferences or on podcasts, writing thought leadership pieces, posting on social media or in any other public forum). Done right, it will improve your personal reputation and improve your career prospects. If you're running a business or plan to start one, this habit will increase your chances of winning new business and attract the best people to come and work with you.

Reasons why you don't do it

For the decade I ran my digital agency, I did almost everything to *avoid* putting myself and my opinions out there. My main issue was a fear of being boring or saying something wrong. I could speak on a stage when I had to, but the idea of making public *thinking* part of my business strategy was at best an indulgence and, at worst, a potential embarrassment.

Experimentation: design and test

But I learned the power of sharing my ideas, both for my personal development and, more importantly, for creating value for the businesses and people I work with.

Reasons why you should do it

It's a good use of time. Thinking in public requires articulating the value you create, and doing so will spark new opportunities as you develop a reputation for clear thinking and effective communication.

It's effective. When you start publishing online, don't focus on total numbers of views or clicks, but rather on how many of your specific target audience you meaningfully engage. That means being very clear about who you're talking to and what's important to them.

Concentrate on how you can help answer the questions they care about in a way they'll remember. Digital platforms allow you to engage individuals at scale, but those people want to hear genuine, well-considered thinking from a real human being. You!

Your point of view matters. Imposter syndrome rears its ugly head in many areas of our work/lives, but no more so than when it comes to public thinking. So focus on your niche. Don't try to copy the ideas of others, because people quickly see through it. What do you know that others don't that'll help you frame those problems differently? Your experiences and points of view are unique, so share them!

Failing to be bold is far riskier in the long run than failing to share your thoughts with the world. If you're afraid of looking stupid, the easiest way to get over that fear is to reframe it. Flip it around. How will you feel if you don't achieve your potential because you didn't give something a try?

How to get started

1. Be clear about who you'll be talking to and what they're interested in.
2. Focus on your niche – where do your skills and interests overlap to help you tell a story to your audience? Remember, it's just a starting point, so don't get too hung up on it.
3. Start collecting ideas whenever they come to you and jot them down in a notepad or a note-taking app on your phone.
4. Begin adding thoughtful social media comments on topics relevant to your niche.
5. Experiment with sharing something significant that's happened in your workday using different

Experimentation: design and test

media – you may be more comfortable with audio or video than writing, for example.
6. Don't be scared about offering an informed opinion.
7. Keep going even if there's little engagement initially. It takes time.

Once you've nurtured an audience and consistently demonstrated the value you offer them, writing a newsletter can prove lucrative, especially if monetized through sponsorship and adjacent businesses.

Creating a content flywheel

The aha moment came for me when I realized that two things I enjoyed doing in my spare time – reading and listening to podcasts – were the starting point to reimagine the next step in my career. Once I began, the momentum kept building and I keep my content flywheel turning through:

- **Listening:** I don't just listen to the same few podcasts on rotation. I introduce new shows on wildly different themes each week to broaden my insights.

- **Reading:** When I hear something I like, I find the speaker's work, online or in their books. Reading remains the fastest way to deepen understanding and knowledge.
- **Recording:** If I'm curious about someone's work, I invite them onto my podcast. Shaping the questions based on my curiosity accelerates my learning and means the guest's experience is unique rather than following the formula of other shows.
- **Writing:** Conversations reveal multiple insights, which feed into my newsletter and now provide a reservoir of ideas for digital and analogue content.
- **Iterating:** I use data to analyse which ideas resonate best, and this helps uncover the themes I should focus on, guiding my discovery of possible new collaborators through more podcast listening.

Continually creating and testing is critical, and your curiosity will keep the flywheel turning. But best of all, when you share your thinking in public, people will be drawn to you, creating the opportunity to build your community.

Experimentation: design and test

So what? Over to you…

1. What small, low-risk experiment could you design this week to test an idea you've been curious about?

2. What feedback or data will you look for to measure whether your experiment is moving you closer to your goal?

Experimentation: design and test

3. What unique skills, perspectives or passions could you combine to create a niche that excites you and stands out to others? How can you start testing its potential?

Day 7
Community: connecting and collaborating

It's never been easier to find your 'tribe' online. You can now collaborate with others in new creative ways and accelerate your learning based on the experiences of people from different backgrounds.

Cultivating a community requires us to build new relationships, which inevitably means you need to start *networking* your arse off. But if you hate networking, don't panic!

The case for networking

My podcast has become a beautiful illustration of how and why I've fundamentally changed my view

Community: connecting and collaborating

of networks since I started my career transition; it's all about creating meaningful connections. I made a conscious effort to interact with anyone whose work I was interested in. Quickly realizing these conversations were worth capturing, I started a podcast, leading to dozens more new relationships and, ultimately, this book. What began as an exercise in satisfying my curiosity led to something much greater.

Limiting yourself to a close-knit group for counsel can place unnecessary constraints on your future opportunities. Look at gaining a broader perspective from a more diverse collection of people.

While it's critical to cultivate a robust and diverse network, it's also true that deeper relationships, built on trust and understanding, can inspire confidence and action. The challenge is to find the right combination of each.

Mapping the people you spend time with – writing down their names and drawing lines to connect any that know each other – can help you uncover insights like how interconnected (or not) your network is, who you get new ideas and opportunities from, which groups influence your habits and behaviours and, importantly, how resilient your support network is. Just as you scrutinize your personal development

– your skills and experience – do the same for your relationships.

If I'm curious about a subject and appreciate someone's ideas, I write a concise and thoughtful note to them – easy. In many cases, they are open to chatting about their work and mine. I've curated and shared the information I've gathered in this way with my *Future Work/Life* community. In turn, this has led to more people introducing themselves and to me making introductions to others in my growing network.

Whether you're building a network or transforming loose connections into committed communities, these relationships will drive your Work/Life Flywheel.

Connection and collaboration

But what's the impact of swapping face-to-face interactions for virtual meetings? Does the lack of a shared physical experience take the joy out of our relationships?

It could, but luckily there are other ways we can create connection. Thank goodness for the internet.

Community: connecting and collaborating

Analogue and digital connections

There are plenty of exciting ways to build connections. You could:

- replicate a team environment with the people you work alongside in flexible working spaces (just without shared clients and colleagues)
- arrange regular interactions with a select group of industry colleagues or a mastermind group
- join online communities and take the relationships offline to meet in person

There are more and more digital courses, focusing on every conceivable topic and area of interest, and when you work through a programme as a group, you're more likely to put into practice what you've learned. It's both possible and desirable to cultivate relationships that offer genuine connection and a sense of relatedness, something we miss out on when working only in isolation.

Maximizing the value of group experiences

To get the most out of collaborative sessions, try creating the following conditions:

- **Shared goals:** Make sure everyone understands and is aligned with the session's objectives.
- **The right level of complexity:** The challenge should be significant enough to engage everyone's full attention but not so complicated that achieving it is impossible in the time available.
- **Full attention:** There's no taking a call mid-meeting and certainly no responding to emails.
- **Equal participation:** Not only should everyone's voice be heard, but the whole group should share a common language, meaning you need a relatively level playing field when it comes to subject matter expertise.
- **Open communication and close listening:** You need to listen carefully to what everyone is saying. Collaboration is an opportunity to create new perspectives, not reinforce opinions.
- **'Yes' culture:** In a collaborative session, it's far more effective to build on someone's point, not shoot it down.
- **Novelty and predictability:** Ensure that ideas are always progressing. Introducing

something unexpected can force everyone to pay close attention.
- **Blending egos:** Leave your ego at the door. Trust each other to find the best solution.
- **Control:** We should aim for the right balance of openness to others' opinions while maintaining confidence that we can express our own.

Rather than seeing digital interactions as barriers to building connections, contemplate the opportunities they present instead – not least how cooperating in exciting ways unlocks the potential for monetizing our experience and interests.

The cooperation economy

As work evolves, our 'soft' skills – how we communicate and collaborate with others, including an ability to quickly adapt and get up to speed on the priorities of a project – will become ever more important.

Writer and venture capitalist Packy McCormick identifies 'Liquid Super Teams' – fluid groups of people who come together to leverage their highly specialized sets of skills – as the foundation of the emerging 'cooperation economy'.[10] These groups aren't bound by location or even time zone, but combine because their expertise and philosophy are complementary. They represent supercharged new possibilities for your career.

Since the commitment required from each individual is low, these teams attract a broad set of talented people. They do away with the costs of a traditional organization, creating more value for customers. Also, since groups of freelancers and solopreneurs have their own audience and proven systems, the liquid structure benefits from an expanded network and community.

Pooling expertise globally also increases the chances of cognitive diversity. People's background, upbringing, education and interests all play a part in how they think. Their lived experience contributes to their outlook, beliefs and how they approach subjects like problem-solving and creativity. All of this is why it makes career and business sense to prioritize creating a diverse and inclusive team.

The evolution of teams

One of the beauties of controlling your pattern of work and having agency over which clients you work with is that you can gradually shape your own

Community: connecting and collaborating

work/life. This is why more and more small business owners, freelancers or contractors are coming together in formal or informal collectives. They create the communities they need in the absence of a full-time employer. And that matters.

Communities can provide a bridge to the freedom and opportunities you're searching for. Joining an existing community can be a great way to build your confidence and get you started.

However you choose to nurture your community, you'll find it brings you the chance to experiment and build new connections and provides an incredible opportunity to keep learning.

So what? Over to you…

1. Who in your current network inspires you, and how could you reach out to deepen that connection or start a meaningful conversation?

2. What specific steps could you take to expand your network to include more diverse perspectives and experiences?

3. How can you create or join a community that aligns with your goals to foster collaboration, learning and growth?

Day 8
Ongoing success

It's tempting to measure your success against that of your peers. But it's more fulfilling to focus your energy on creating a work/life that gives *you* purpose and in which *you* feel like you're making progress.

The multi-stage life

The idea of the average person working for 40 years and then retiring to a quiet life is behind us as we are required to constantly reskill and adapt. A longer, healthier life will allow people to work until much later, with these years scattered with sabbaticals and periods of more intense education.

Longer lives will also lead to more people starting their own businesses, developing portfolio careers as they master new skills, and developing broader networks. Consistently starting new pursuits such as courses and entrepreneurial ventures will expose us to more diverse collaborators.

Ongoing learning

Learning doesn't stop!

- Stay open-minded to new opportunities and focus your time on learning about things that align with your values and purpose.
- Use flow to maximize the rate at which you learn, and understand how stories create connections between people.
- Experiment with new ideas, and don't be afraid to make mistakes, as these often lead to the biggest changes.
- Constantly push yourself to meet new people with different perspectives and backgrounds who'll teach you about new topics and ways of thinking.

The Work/Life Flywheel provides a model to help you achieve and exceed your potential. Your focus should be on the small actions you can take each day, which compound over time. By constantly pushing yourself slightly harder each day, before you know it you'll hit the sweet spot and experience the benefits of compound growth in your career.

Systems and the importance of teaching yourself

There's huge value in formal education and structured courses, but there's also much to be learned from building a community, engaging with experts and building relationships with people who have varying experiences and divergent perspectives. There comes a point, though, when the difference between ordinary and legendary is what *you* do.

And there's a (long) word for the process of doing this: *autodidacticism*.

To be autodidactic means mastering a subject without the guidance of a teacher. This represents the most significant opportunity to differentiate yourself from others. Only you can:

- determine the subjects you're most interested in learning about
- decide on the depth to which you'll dig to discover more
- choose how much time to spend doing it and when

Reimagine Your Career

Entrepreneur Justin Welsh, for example, realized that he needed to make significant changes in his work/life. He left a highly paid job to go it alone and has since built a diversified portfolio of one-person internet businesses. Nobody showed Justin how to do this. He worked it out for himself by:

- making an informed decision about how and where to spend his time most effectively (*the hypothesis*)
- learning the skills to be able to communicate his ideas (*through copywriting*)
- applying the principles of public thinking (see Day 6) to market his new businesses (*sharing his point of view*)
- being relentlessly clear about where he was going but flexible about how he got there (*consistency*)

Justin's approach is the perfect example of a Work/Life Flywheel that, as time progresses, builds more and more momentum.

(He was also careful to carve out time to step back and reflect by going on long walks with his wife and ensuring he spent time away from the computer with friends and loved ones between Fridays and Sundays.)

Ongoing success

By combining autodidacticism with well-thought-out systems, Justin has redesigned a more sustainable and rewarding work/life.

Necessity is the mother of invention

Chronic insomnia led Kathrin Hamm to quit her job to found a company – Bearaby – selling weighted blankets. Arguably this was a strange decision. She had spent years attaining a PhD and had a great job at a world-renowned organization, making a real difference to people's lives. So what led her to take such a risk?

It's one of the clearest cases of 'necessity is the mother of invention' that I've come across. Kathrin decided that *she* was the person to create a new category of product. Giving herself a 12-month deadline to see if she could make it work, she set about trying to produce a natural weighted blanket that was both practical and good-looking.

Community reciprocity

Switching from being an international development economist to a start-up founder certainly put Kathrin outside her comfort zone. Fortunately, she discovered a community open to welcoming her into the fold and supporting her development. In the same spirit, she now gives back to her extended network, encouraging others with their entrepreneurial endeavours.

Following your curiosity

It can feel impossible to work out what to do next after being buried deep in a particular field of work or having established a reputation and expertise in one industry. It can be challenging to remember who you really are.

Without overthinking it, consider the following questions:

- When you're not thinking directly about your job, what are you doing?
- If you have an hour to yourself, what do you look forward to?
- Picture a week away from your current job. What sort of activities would you enjoy?
- Think for a moment about what you were chatting about at a party or over dinner.
- If I was to ask your best friend or partner what you love to learn about, what would they say?

- What interests do you feel like you haven't had time for over the past five years but would love to dig into again?

You can get so bogged down with the significance of 'discovering your purpose' that it puts you off even starting. Remember, don't overcomplicate it. Concentrate on things that you enjoy and make you feel good.

Here are two ideas to get you started:

1. **Track your daily highlights:** If you write down a couple of daily highlights every evening, you will start to notice patterns. Whatever it is, do more of it!
2. **Notice how you spend your time:** It might seem odd to incorporate a personal interest into your work, but perhaps your love of history, for example, will bring a different perspective to a client's problem. Bring your unique point of view to the party.

Why curiosity?

When I began redesigning my work/life, I focused on identifying my five guiding principles: autonomy, creativity, curiosity, growth and humour.

Among the many smart and successful people I've interviewed in my research, *curiosity* is one of the most recognizable characteristics. Some specifically reference it. Others implicitly display it in how they discuss their interests and passion for work. It's often a value that motivates them to persist even when the going gets tough.

Why is curiosity so valuable?

Psychologists talk about the 'information deficit' view of curiosity: you realize there's something you don't know, and you want to figure it out.

- If you've got no idea what you don't know, you're not curious.
- If you think you know everything, you're not curious.
- If you know something and you also know that there are gaps, that's when you get very curious.

A multi-stage life means we'll have more than one career. While factors outside our control drive some changes in work, we are in charge of how we respond to them. In these moments, it also pays to be aware of what interests us so that we can spot new ways of channelling our curiosity.

Storytelling and experimentation

Jeff Kofman had a 30-year career in the public eye, gaining a reputation as one of the world's leading war correspondents. While he was passionate about passing on some of the knowledge he'd accumulated over those years, he didn't envisage permanently settling into a teaching role. Instead, he followed his curiosity.

In 2013, he was introduced to a team that had developed a solution to align text with audio. Jeff didn't understand the technology, but he understood the pain of transcribing interviews all too well.

'Would this work if you used automated speech-to-text to transcribe it,' he inquired, 'and made the spoken word searchable?'

'It's an interesting idea,' said the developers. 'We could try.'

At this point, Jeff's second career as an accidental entrepreneur began.

Eight years on, Jeff was leading a fast-growing business. Jeff didn't know much about entrepreneurship, but he did know about storytelling and, in particular, why solving this problem was a story that people in his former role would want to hear.

As he put together the business plan for his company (Trint) he felt well out of his depth. He'd never managed anyone and could barely use a spreadsheet, and when it came to pitching, he had no idea about how to speak the lingo.

So he focused on the lessons he'd learned from his career as a reporter. He used his interviewing skills to ask questions to find out things that might have been obvious to other people but which, to him, served as a crash course in business and entrepreneurship. He embraced his lack of start-up experience rather than letting it get in the way.

Jeff built a second career by letting his curiosity, passion and vision guide him. Motivated to learn as much as possible as quickly as possible, he achieved a period of unforeseen personal growth.

Whatever stage of your career and life you are in, it never hurts to love what you do. And it's never too late to take on a new challenge.

So what? Over to you…

1. Which daily activities or hobbies consistently bring you joy, and how might you integrate one of these into your work or career?

2. What specific skills or knowledge gaps are holding you back from pursuing a new opportunity, and who or what could help you start addressing them this week?

3. What is one concrete experiment you could run to test whether a personal interest could grow into a new career direction or side project?

Day 9
Time to pause

Every athlete knows that overtraining can lead to peaking too soon and lacking the endurance to stay the course; work is no different. If we were to design our ideal training regime, would it include staring into a screen for hours on end, day after day? Would we work flat out, every day, only taking the odd week off at random times throughout the year?

Nope.

Physical and mental endurance

From the perspective of high performance at work, we massively underestimate the value of pacing. For many, there's little consideration of how to plan the best structure for the working day to optimize for the

Time to pause

peaks in performance, let alone planning for a longer time horizon.

1. During the average week, you may need to prioritize key client presentations, write a new white paper or train a group of new recruits. Instead of just cramming these vital activities randomly into your calendar, plan around them.
2. Ensure you don't have hours of video calls throughout the day beforehand, and give yourself ample time just before a session starts to compose your thoughts and focus.
3. Allow time to balance these periods of intense work with more rest – perhaps even scheduling a holiday or a few days off immediately afterwards. While our work/lives aren't as predictable as the sporting calendar, most people can identify their busier times throughout the year in advance, so incorporate this into your planning.
4. Achieving peak performance requires thinking of yourself as an elite athlete, taking rest and recovery seriously.

The power of sleep

Staying fit and healthy is one part of the puzzle, but make sure you take the time to recover from physical exertion too – a vital component of your recovery is sleep. A lack of sleep leaves you cognitively impaired, which increases the chances of making mistakes and producing lower-quality work in the long run.

As a parent who's been sleep - deprived for most of the past decade, I rarely feel entirely well rested. However, I've learned to adapt my behaviour.

During those periods where lack of sleep is unavoidable, try the following:

1. As far as possible, stick to more routine tasks rather than those that require creativity and innovation, which are more vulnerable to poor decision-making.
2. Explain the situation to friends and colleagues. Most people understand and are willing to help out and share the load – the sign of a great team is one that works together during challenging times.
3. Lean on the advice of others to sanity-check your ideas.
4. Plus, while the amount of sleep you get is cumulatively important, you don't have to get it all in one go.

When we don't get our 'eight hours', it creates anxiety, thus reducing our chances of sleeping well the next night – the result is a vicious circle. The truth is that the body is very resilient and can cope well with periods of little sleep. However, it's essential to allow yourself the time, where possible, to make a dent in that deficit.

Making up for lost sleep

I introduced a daytime sleep into my life in 2020, and while it can't replace the total number of hours lost at night, it gives me the boost I need to get through the afternoon productively.

The trick to effective napping is to limit sleep to no less than 10 minutes and no more than 20. Precede the nap with a coffee or cup of tea, which gives you a double-kick when you wake up since the caffeine takes around 25 minutes to kick in.

Why are we still talking about sleep?

Human characteristics like creativity will become ever more critical in a future of work marked by ever more automation. How we think about problems and navigate our way through life will be more important than learning facts. Better sleep contributes to better mood, which, neurologically, helps us consider less obvious solutions to challenging problems.

I can't pretend that I have the answer to a permanently positive mood or a perfect night's sleep, but these should help:

1. A short *gratitude practice* of only five minutes releases dopamine and serotonin, significantly improving our mood.
2. *Physical exercise* releases dopamine and endorphins into your brain, leaving you feeling happier, more energetic and with enhanced productivity.
3. As well as the stress-relieving benefits of *getting outside and into nature*, this also helps with 'attention restoration', restoring depleted attention circuits, countering the effects of mental fatigue and burn-out while fostering an open, meditative mindset.

For every two hours spent awake consuming new information and forming new memories, our brains should go 'offline' for an hour to process the thoughts. But life doesn't always go to plan.

So if you're getting less than seven hours, like me, here are some ways to limit the damage.

Time to pause

Flow and recovery

We talked about flow triggers in Day 5, but did you know there are four stages to the flow cycle? They are:

1. **Struggle:** When we initially immerse ourselves in a problem, taking on new information and pushing ourselves to discover more, it can feel tough. This is a good thing – keep pushing on.
2. **Release:** When you really hit the wall and can't do any more, that's when you stop and step away from the problem entirely.
3. **Flow:** Only when you return to the task at hand do you enter a flow state.
4. **Recovery:** Being in flow takes a toll on the central nervous system and body, tapping into the energy and resources we build in preparation, so it's essential to step away afterwards and take some time to recover.

So rest and recovery are a vital part of doing your best work. There's no glory in overwork and burnout.

Emptying the stress bucket

Nik Whitfield had been battling chronic pain for years before he began using body scan meditation and journalling. The meditation was his first acknowledgement of the acute physical pain he was experiencing. Journalling was a way of 'expunging it'. Recognizing that he'd experienced trauma in his life, he began journalling to write about the things he had buried inside him – anxiety, humiliation, anger, resentment, any kind of negative emotion.

Within a month of implementing these new habits, 90% of the pain had gone.

His business has flourished in the years since. Most importantly for Nik, a positive approach to well-being is a fundamental part of his company's culture and has changed his life.

By taking the time to reflect on the root causes of his pain, he has unlocked new levels of physical fitness and insight that feed directly into the success of his company and his happiness.

Journalling

Most people who describe themselves as 'happy' and 'fulfilled' practise some form of journalling.

Time to pause

The effectiveness of journalling lies in reflection. We encounter vast amounts of information every day and have countless sources of stimuli fighting for our attention and responsibilities stacked on top of each other. Pausing to reflect is crucial to allow our minds and bodies to recover.

Innovation versus invention

Those moments of pause and reflection are where innovation often begins as we create space for our minds to connect ideas and spark creativity. Interestingly, Albert Einstein would sail his boat into the centre of a lake and sit in solitude, searching for inspiration away from the distraction of daily life.

To be innovative is now up there with being 'forward-thinking', being 'smart' and having 'integrity' when businesses talk about their culture and people.

But these words have somewhat lost their meaning.

In *How Innovation Works*, Matt Ridley explains that history has consistently demonstrated innovation happening slowly through testing and tweaking.[11] It requires constant iteration and inevitable failure before you ultimately reach a breakthrough.

While the aha moments may come during periods when we switch our brain off, as with the example of Einstein, by this point the real work has already been done.

Design thinking

Sarah Stein Greenberg and her colleagues teach the principles of design thinking, a process which now informs some of the most brilliant businesses and organizations in the world. Their methodology has five stages:

1. **Empathize:** Empathy allows you to set aside your assumptions and preconceptions to gain insight into the problem you're solving and who you're solving it for.
2. **Define:** After gathering your research, you define the problem from the user's point of view – for example, 'We need to design a new model that empowers people to thrive and grow in work and life.'
3. **Ideate:** When you're clear about the problem, you need to develop as many solutions as possible and start thinking about how you can test whether they'll be effective or not.

4. **Prototype:** During this experimental phase, designers test their hypotheses in the real world. This may involve creating a physical prototype for a product, but it could equally apply to developing a new schedule, a new approach to networking or a new content flywheel.
5. **Test:** Although this is the final stage of the model, designers take an iterative approach, which requires testing, measuring results and then redefining the problem to start once again.

The point is that you consciously design a new way of thinking that provides a platform to build something better. But what does that have to do with pausing and reflection?

From action to inaction

Sarah is clear that action and reflection are inextricably linked. She advocates a form of journalling to help inspire breakthroughs – this is called 'What?/So What?/Now What?'

- **What?** Write down everything that happened before reflecting on what it means.

- **So what?** Why is it important, and why did it feel like something you wanted to capture?
- **Now what?** What do you want to do about it? Is it something you can test, practise or improve on?

Innovation is about designing how we work to optimize for creativity and productivity. It's about providing the opportunity to collaborate with others, creating the conditions for focused work to get into flow and constantly searching for new knowledge. However, it's also about creating moments for reflection every day.

High performance requires the energy to push yourself mentally and physically, so it's critical to counterbalance the exertion with downtime. Passion can lead to burn-out. Its symptoms include:

- Feelings of energy depletion or exhaustion
- Increased mental distance from one's job or feelings of negativism or cynicism related to one's job
- Reduced professional efficacy

The trick to building a sustainable approach to your creative and productive work/life is incorporating downtime into your schedule – not

Time to pause

just hoping for moments of recovery and reflection, but insisting on them.

After all, why do you think Einstein used to sail to the middle of that lake?

Now we've covered how to design your time to allow for reflection and recovery, let's consider how to track your progress.

✏️ So what? Over to you...

1. What regular activities or habits might be contributing to overwork, and how can you redesign them to avoid burn-out?

2. What small adjustments can you make to optimize your daily routine for better mental and physical endurance?

Time to pause

3. Which of these strategies might you use to improve your sleep?

Day 10
Tracking, trusting and taking steps

Andy Ayim takes reflection seriously and has developed a journalling habit that provides him with a unique level of self-awareness and insight.

Since moving to California to work in the tech industry, with all its new terminology and conventions, he has documented his thoughts and feelings every day in a 'tracker'. Alongside his blog, Andy has tracked his progress in his version of a digital journal, recording any significant events and emotions at the end of every day. He's able to use this not just as a tracking tool but also as a resource for new ideas as he regularly analyses the data to help him spot connections between patterns of behaviour and thinking. Through a combination of written notes and images – screenshots of messages or photos of memorable experiences – he has built up a 'second brain'.

Andy's tracker has trained him to pay more attention to the most significant events in his work/life, and crucially it has given him a simple way to monitor and observe his progress.

He has embraced a creative mindset to build communities with whom he shares *his* knowledge, and they also inspire *him* to continually learn. It's no wonder that he has achieved so many substantial breakthroughs so quickly.

Andy has built a perfectly functioning Work/Life Flywheel!

The power of progress

Money and status can sometimes be the main obstacle to changing our work/lives – the so-called 'golden handcuffs'. As we get older and responsibilities stack up, a sense that we have fewer options can become stronger. It may seem impossible to just throw away all your inhibitions and blindly leap into a career move.

But reimagining work needn't be a binary choice – *either* continuing in the same job, at the same employer, working the same hours, *or* quitting. It can be a more incremental process, with small steps all adding up to big change over time.

Good things don't happen overnight. Start small, stay consistent and celebrate the progress you make. Understand what matters to you, develop new habits that enable more creativity, experimentation and learning, and build your network.

Teresa Amabile and Steven Kramer of Harvard Business School have analysed the internal emotions that reflect our day-to-day experiences. They found that the single biggest influence on a sense of fulfilment is a feeling of making progress. Significant events – like closing new client deals – are less important than you'd think.[12]

Unfortunately, our brains are wired to convey negative emotions more powerfully than their positive counterparts, which means you have to consciously reframe setbacks as learning opportunities. For example: 'I didn't get the promotion I wanted, but now I understand what I need to improve on to be successful next time.'

Remember that the work you're doing doesn't need to change the world to be meaningful. It just needs to matter to you. This is why being clear about your values and goals in the first place makes a huge difference. Every time we complete a task or receive feedback that aligns with our purpose, however minor, we give ourselves something to cheer about. So, make sure you do it!

But how?

Micro-journalling

Like any part of your work/life, there's a danger of analysis paralysis – overthinking how or why you're doing something rather than focusing on getting it done. So start small.

Micro-journalling is one habit that has changed my life over the past couple of years. At the end of each day, I spend five minutes noting down answers to the following questions:

1. How do I feel about the day in general – was it productive, frustrating, exciting, sad?
2. What's the main reason for feeling this way?
3. What was my biggest achievement at work?
4. What was my biggest achievement in my personal life?

And, finally, my favourite:

5. What were the most story-worthy moments of the day?

As we scrutinize what has happened during the day – however large or small – we acknowledge the significance of our work. We're placing a marker down by identifying a highlight that demonstrates our progress.

Taking five minutes to think about these five questions has had the following five results for me:

- I have reduced stress and anxiety.
- I can see the progress I'm making.
- I can spot patterns so that I can do more of the good stuff.
- I can see a positive connection between work and life.
- My memory has improved and time feels like it has slowed down – I remember more.

To gain perspective and recognize your progress, take a step back from life's craziness and start tracking your achievements today.

Trusting the process

Like you and so many others, I'm in the middle of a work/life transition.

Fundamentally reconsidering what to do and how to do it isn't easy. There are frequent moments of self-doubt, and the trick is to learn to trust the process. While having a north star can provide motivation and purpose, true satisfaction only comes if we recognize and enjoy the moment we're experiencing right now. The things that we do every day are all that matter.

Despite giving you a model to help you reimagine your work/life, I can't promise you that everything will go exactly to plan. Accepting that can be a relief, so try giving in to the fact that there are some things you can't control and see how you feel. One thing is for sure, something unexpected will emerge, and new opportunities will arise that you would never previously have considered. (I had no idea that redesigning my own work/life would lead to writing this book, for example.)

Giving in to the power of time may seem like giving up, but actually it's the opposite.

It's all about the small decisions

- By remaining open-minded and being clear about my purpose and goals, I recognize that I'm staying true to what matters to me, including relationships, health and things that bring me joy.

- By embracing creativity and understanding the power of stories – my own and those of others – I've realized that life is more colourful and meaningful than I thought.
- At the mid-point of my life (or a little before, if all goes to plan), I finally understand that making progress demands trying new things, even when they don't work – that's how real change happens.
- Perhaps the most significant personal change is that I've grown to love meeting new people and, particularly, learning from them by following my curiosity.
- As I write this, I'm also the fittest I've ever been, physically and mentally, because I no longer compromise on looking after myself.

I've reimagined my career, but I haven't worked out all the answers, which is lucky as there's plenty more of my life to go. Through the examples I've shared with you and the stories of the wonderful people I've written about, I hope you'll be inspired to redesign *your* work/life and take this unprecedented opportunity to grow.

Trust the process, take care of yourself and take the first step.

So what? Over to you…

1. How can you create a simple, daily practice to reflect on your progress and achievements?

2. What is one area of your work/life where you could let go of overthinking, and instead trust the process to unfold?

Tracking, trusting and taking steps

3. What is one 'small decision' you could make today that aligns with your values and moves you a little closer to your goals?

Conclusion: sharing your ideas

Alongside the incredible new connections and opportunities I've created over the past couple of years, writing has positively impacted my mental health, my relationships and even my perception of time.

Writing has influenced my work/life in five profound ways:

1. **Rediscovering my purpose and identity:** Writing helped me align what matters most – my unique skills, availability of opportunities and ability to provide for my family.
2. **Defeating imposter syndrome:** Simply writing down my feelings helps quieten my 'monkey mind' and expunge self-doubt.
3. **Exploring new ideas:** Free-writing and long-form articles both expose things I don't yet clearly understand and consolidate my expertise.

Conclusion: sharing your ideas

4. **Creating a progress portfolio:** Documenting my work is the secret to successfully measuring and accelerating my progress.
5. **Slowing time:** I've built an external memory log by recording one key achievement and a story-worthy moment every day, meaning the days no longer blur into one.

If there's only one lesson I can share with you based on my experience, it's to put your ideas out there in the world. Once I got over my fear of doing that, it opened my eyes and countless doors.

Endnotes

[1] L. Gratton, *Redesigning Work: How to transform your organisation and make hybrid work for everyone* (2022).

[2] B. Feiler, *Life Is in the Transitions: Mastering change at any age* (2020).

[3] K. Neff, *Self Compassion: The proven power of being kind to yourself* (2011).

[4] S. Friedman and A. Westring, *Parents Who Lead: The leadership approach you need to parent with purpose, fuel your career, and create a richer life* (2020).

[5] R. Moss Kanter, 'Change is hardest in the middle' in *Harvard Business Review* (12 August 2009). Available from https://hbr.org/2009/08/change-is-hardest-in-the-middl

[6] Friedman and Westring, *Parents Who Lead*.

[7] P. J. Zak, 'Why your brain loves good storytelling' in *Harvard Business Review* (28 October 2014). Available from https://hbr.org/2014/10/why-your-brain-loves-good-storytelling

[8] M. Dicks, *Storyworthy: Engage, teach, persuade, and change your life through the power of storytelling* (2018).

[9] D. Cable, *Alive at Work: The neuroscience of helping your people love what they do* (2018).

Endnotes

[10] P. McCormick, *The cooperation economy*, Not Boring (7 June 2021). Available from www.notboring.co/p/the-cooperation-economy-#:~:text=That's%20a%20Liquid%20Super%20Team,optionality%2C%20and%20everyone%20has%20upside

[11] M. Ridley, *How Innovation Works: And why it flourishes in freedom* (2020).

[12] T. Amabile and S. Kramer, *The Progress Principle: Using small wins to ignite joy, engagement, and creativity at work* (2011).

Enjoyed this?
Then you'll love…

Work/Life Flywheel: Harness the work revolution and reimagine your career without fear by Ollie Henderson

Business Book Awards 2024 Finalist

> 'The system you need to make bold changes in your career'
> – Daniel H. Pink

We're experiencing a work revolution with an unprecedented opportunity to reimagine how, when and where we do what we do. Now is the perfect time to take more control over your work/life and maybe even finally take the leap into going it alone, whether by starting your own business or turning your passion into a career.

Ollie Henderson shares the lessons he's learned by interviewing entrepreneurs, business leaders and world-renowned experts on his chart-topping podcast

Enjoyed this? Then you'll love…

Future Work/Life. Forget work/life balance, the secret to navigating a career transition today is to create a flywheel that aligns all parts of your work and life and harness small wins to help build the momentum you need to succeed.

- Take control of your long-term future using a proven step-by-step process.
- Develop the confidence to transform your career by focusing on becoming an expert in your niche.
- Adopt a creative and experimental approach to your work/life that delivers consistent, measurable results.
- Cultivate a network of global collaborators to support your transition and generate new opportunities.

Experienced founder and CEO Ollie Henderson pivoted his career while juggling the pleasures and pressures of raising a young family. He believes work/life balance is a myth. Rather than seeing career and personal life as two opposing forces, Ollie argues that the secret is to design an integrated approach that allows them to work in harmony.

Other 6-Minute Smarts titles

Building Great Teams (based on *Workshop Culture* by Alison Coward)

Do Change Better (based on *How to be a Change Superhero* by Lucinda Carney)

How to be Happy at Work (based on *My Job Isn't Working!* by Michael Brown)

How to Get to Know Your Customer (based on *Do Penguins Eat Peaches?* by Katie Tucker)

The Listening Leader (based on *The Listening Shift* by Janie Van Hool)

Mastering People Management (based on *Mission: To Manage* by Marianne Page)

No-Nonsense PR (based on *Hype Yourself* by Lucy Werner)

Present Like a Pro (based on *Executive Presentations* by Jacqui Harper)

Sales Made Simple (based on *More Sales Please* by Sara Nasser Dalrymple)

The Speed Storytelling Toolkit (based on *Exposure* by Felicity Cowie)

Write to Think (based on *Exploratory Writing* by Alison Jones)

Look out for more titles coming soon! Visit www.practicalinspiration.com for all our latest titles.